W9-CPO-479

Let's Work It Out™

What to Do When Your Family Is on Welfare

Rachel Lynette

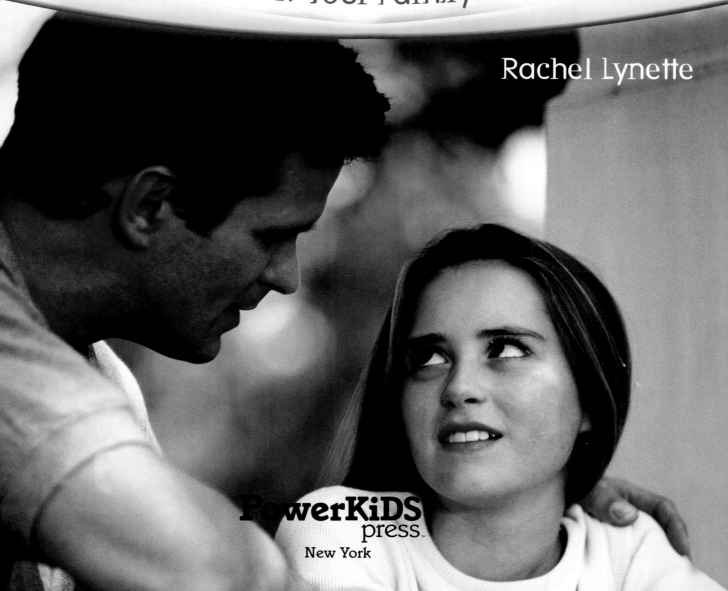

PowerKiDS press™

New York

Published in 2010 by The Rosen Publishing Group, Inc.
29 East 21st Street, New York, NY 10010

First Edition

Editor: Joanne Randolph
Layout Design: Julio Gil
Photo Researcher: Jessica Gerweck

Photo Credits: Cover Lonny Kalfus/Getty Images; pp. 4, 12, 14, 16, 18 Shutterstock.com; p. 6 Andy Sacks/Getty Images; p. 8 Andersen Ross/Getty Images; p. 10 © www.iStockphoto.com/Chris Schmidt; p. 20 © Assunta Del Buono/age fotostock.

Library of Congress Cataloging-in-Publication Data

Lynette, Rachel.
   What to do when your family is on welfare / Rachel Lynette.
      p. cm. — (Let's work it out)
   Includes index.
   ISBN 978-1-4358-9337-5 (library binding) — ISBN 978-1-4358-9762-5 (pbk.) — ISBN 978-1-4358-9763-2 (6-pack)
   1. Public welfare—Juvenile literature. I. Title.
   HV11.L96 2010
   362.7086'9420973—dc22

                                        2009019863

Manufactured in the United States of America

CPSIA Compliance Information: Batch #WW10PK: For Further Information contact Rosen Publishing, New York, New York at 1-800-237-9932

Contents

If your family needs to apply for welfare, ask your mom to explain what is happening and what it will mean for your family.

What Is Welfare?

When Cory was in second grade, his mom and dad got divorced. Cory lived with his mom. Even though Cory's mom had a job, she did not make very much money. She worked hard, but there never seemed to be enough money. Soon there was not enough money for food or to pay the rent. Cory's mom needed help taking care of herself and Cory. She got help by **applying** for welfare.

Welfare is a group of **government** programs that help families that are in need. The programs help families by giving them money, food, and help with medical care and housing. Welfare programs also help people get jobs.

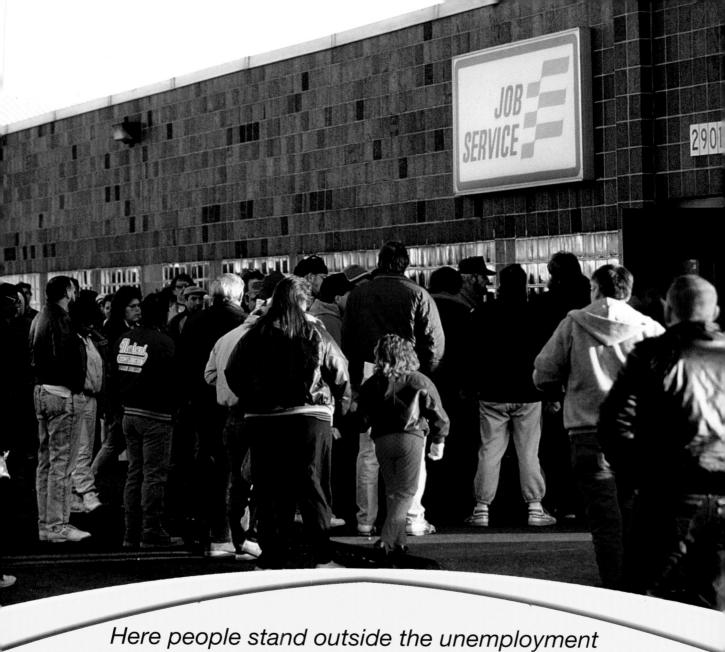

Here people stand outside the unemployment office after losing their jobs. Unemployment is a welfare program that helps people find new jobs.

Why Do We Need Welfare?

Most parents earn money by working. If your parent loses his job, your family may not have enough money. Sometimes a parent cannot work because he gets **injured** or sick. Even people who have jobs sometimes need welfare. People with jobs that do not pay very much may need welfare even though they work hard!

Single parents may also need welfare. It is hard to take care of children and work full-time without a partner to help. A single mother who works must pay someone to care for her children. She must also miss work when her children are sick.

Only some foods are covered by SNAP and WIC, so families on these programs must choose what they buy carefully.

SNAP and WIC

Some families may not have enough money for food. There is a welfare program, called Supplemental Nutrition Assistance Program, or SNAP, which helps these families. This program used to be called the Food Stamp Program.

Families who use SNAP get a card from the government. The card looks just like a credit card. When a person goes to the store, she can use the card to pay for food. SNAP cards can be used only to buy food.

Women, Infants, and Children, or WIC, is another government program. WIC helps pregnant women and mothers with babies and young children by giving them **nutritious** food for their families.

These people are learning new computer skills in a program paid for by TANF. New job skills will help these people find work.

Only for a Little While

A big part of welfare is a program called Temporary Assistance for Needy Families, or TANF. TANF helps families by giving them money. TANF also helps people get good jobs so they can take care of themselves and get off welfare.

One way TANF helps adults is by teaching them **skills** that are needed to get good jobs. When a person has more skills, he can get a job that pays more money. TANF can also give people **transportation** to get to and from a job. Another way TANF can help is by giving parents money for childcare. When people get good jobs, they do not need TANF anymore!

Worrying about money can be stressful for your parents. If your parents are fighting, remember that they are not angry at you.

A Stressful Time for Everyone

Being on welfare can be **stressful** for a family. Even if your family is getting payments from TANF, there still may not be enough money for many things. You may have to go without new clothes, school supplies, or your favorite foods. Your family may even have to move to a smaller house or apartment.

Your parents may feel stressed because they are worried about money. They may feel **ashamed** because they need help. When people are stressed, they sometimes get angry more easily. If it seems like your parents are always angry, remember, it is not your fault. They are just really stressed!

This boy is helping his family by raking the leaves. Every job you do is one less your parents have to do, and you will feel good about helping out.

Be a Stress Stopper

Stress may seem like a grown-up problem, but there are some ways that you can help your parents feel better. One of the best things you can do is have a positive **attitude**. Having a positive attitude means not complaining, even when there is not enough money for things you want or need.

Another good thing you can do is find ways to help around the house. Can you do the dishes or fold clothes? Remember, though, that it is not your job to take care of your family. Do what you can, but do not feel bad if your parents are still stressed. Just know that you are doing your part to help and **encourage** your family.

If you work hard at school, you will not have as much time to worry about what other people are thinking about you.

Dealing at School

If you are on welfare, you may feel different from the other kids at school. You might have to wear old clothes and shoes. Your parents may not be able to pay for extra things like field trips and uniforms. You may even get teased by your classmates. You may feel ashamed or **embarrassed**.

It can help to remember that you have no reason to feel ashamed. Welfare exists because there are so many families who need help to make ends meet. Your family is not the only one going through hard times. Your parents are doing their best. Try to do your best, too. Work hard at doing well in school. Getting good grades is more important than having new clothes.

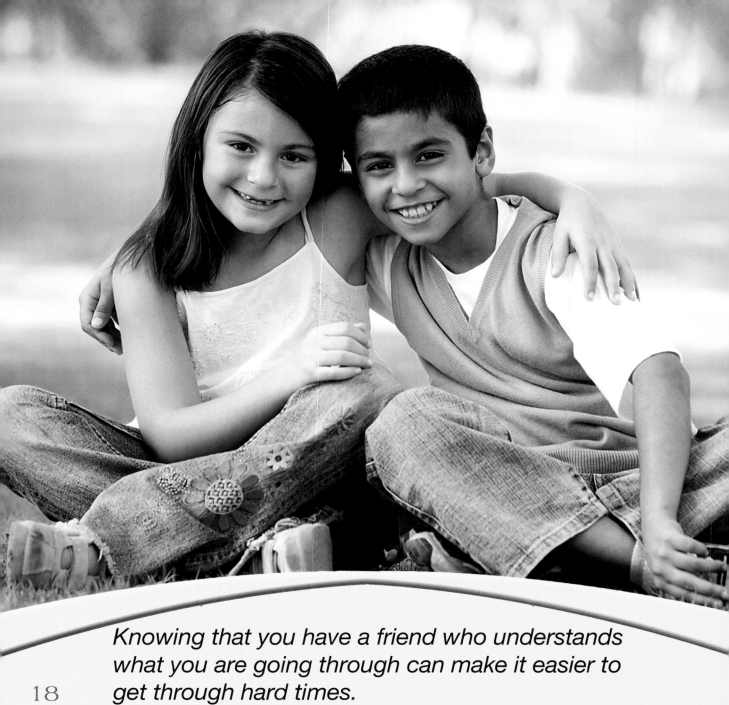

Knowing that you have a friend who understands what you are going through can make it easier to get through hard times.

Friends Can Help

It is always nice to have friends, but when times are hard, friends are even more important. Having fun with your friends is a great way to make yourself feel better. You do not need to feel bad about having fun. Even when things are hard at home, it is okay to enjoy yourself. If you are feeling happy, you will help your family feel happier, too.

You do not have to tell your friends that your family is on welfare. However, it can help to have someone with whom you can talk. You may want to tell one or two of your closest friends. If they are good friends, they will understand. Talking to a friend about the hard things in your life can help you feel better.

A counselor can also help you find healthy ways to deal with what is happening.

Counselors Can Help

It is okay to feel worried when your family is going through a hard time. Sometimes, it can help to talk to an adult, such as a teacher or relative, about your problems. Some welfare programs can help you find a **counselor** with whom you can talk. You may also be able to talk to a counselor at your school or church.

A counselor may be able to help you and your family deal with stress. Remember, a counselor is someone you can trust. It is okay to tell a counselor about your feelings. A counselor can help you see that what is happening is not your fault.

Everyone Needs Help Sometimes

It was hard when Cory and his mom went on welfare. They had to move into a smaller apartment. Cory's mom was worried about money all the time, too. Then she started a job-training program to learn new skills. One day, Cory's mom got a new, higher-paying job! Soon they no longer needed welfare.

Everyone needs help sometimes. If your family needs help from welfare right now, that is okay. Yours is not the only family that needs it. Thousands of other families are on welfare, too. Someday things may get better, and your family will not need welfare anymore. Just think of welfare as a way to help your family get back on its feet.

Glossary

applying (uh-PLY-ing) Asking for something.

ashamed (uh-SHAYMD) Uncomfortable because of something you did or something that happened.

attitude (A-tih-tood) A person's outlook or way of looking at things.

counselor (KOWN-seh-ler) Someone who talks with people about their feelings and problems and who gives advice.

embarrassed (em-BAR-usd) Felt shame or uneasiness.

encourage (in-KUR-ij) To give hope, cheer, or certainty.

government (GUH-vern-mint) The people who make laws and run a state or a country.

injured (IN-jurd) Hurt.

nutritious (noo-TRIH-shus) Having to do with healthy food.

skills (SKILZ) Abilities or things that help one do a job well.

stressful (STRES-ful) Causing worry or bad feelings.

transportation (tranz-per-TAY-shun) A way of traveling from one place to another.

Index

Web Sites

Due to the changing nature of Internet links, PowerKids Press has developed an online list of Web sites related to the subject of this book. This site is updated regularly. Please use this link to access the list:

www.powerkidslinks.com/lwio/welfare/